Letters to the Universe

by

Debbie-Ann M. Smith

RoseDog❖Books

PITTSBURGH, PENNSYLVANIA 15238

RoseDog Books
585 Alpha Drive
Suite 103
Pittsburgh, PA 15238
Visit our website at *www.rosedogbookstore.com*

ISBN: 978-1-4809-6797-7
eISBN: 978-1-4809-6774-8

Foreword

I started writing poems as a teenager in high school. I remember my first poem (which I still have, though it's not included in this collection), titled "Am I the Middle Man." This first collection consists mostly of poems written as a teenager, me trying to figure out life, developing my mantras for living. What you will find in this collection is mixed. Although I have a Christian upbringing, you will see that I have included my mistakes and lessons, some in detail and others not so much. I have always reached out to God for strength; He has always given me answers or pointed me in the direction I should go. However, I have a thing for the scenic route, but I always end up where I am supposed to be. I just ask that you remember that I am not a professional writer; this is my hobby and my first time putting my poetry out in public. I wish to improve with each work I create and give to you, but I also wish to give God praise and glory for giving me this talent. I have always wanted to publish a book, but I had no idea what it would be about. My goal was to publish something deep, thought provoking, and just plain AWESOME by the age of thirty. Well, thirty has come and gone. I guess life happened again…and again, and again, and other priorities took precedence; now here I am at thirty-five. I finally got my bachelor's in occupational leadership and learning (yay me!), I met a fantastic fellow (whose name shall not be mentioned), and I am staring down the barrel of retirement in seven years. How did I get to this point? I have heard how good my poetry was since I began writing, but I never took those words seriously (what a shame). As I started to figure out my self-worth, I began to allow myself to believe the nice things people said about me. And this time, the lucky fool who complimented my writing was my "fantastic fellow"! Months into our roller-coaster (I am the roller and he is the coaster) friendship, I did research on self-publishing and discovered how easy it is. And that is how I got to this point.

My goal from here out is to continue to write and develop my words and works and continue to self-publish after retirement. I plan to travel and chronicle those travels in poetry and pictures. So I have come to the best part of this intro: the ending! My son Jhordan, who has been the spice of my life since I first felt him do the Congo on my bladder. He is the best son this mom could ask for (just ask my friends who used to babysit him). He has made me so damned proud (and he is only thirteen). I can only imagine what is to follow, but this work is for him. To show him that anything is possible if you apply yourself, and to encourage him to pursue his passion with ferocity... and to follow in Mommy's example. I want to live by example for my son, as my mother did for me. I need to hail my two older brothers, who both have encouraged me to just be myself and do what makes me happy. They are all the family I have left! And I intend to make them proud. I have to thank so many people, but I will place that at the end because I do want you to get to the poems. I hope you find something in these words that you identify with.

Adolescent Musings

Easier Said Than Done

There is a lesson of value
we have come to learn one way or another.
We all have good intentions,
and in our heart we yearn to help our fallen brother
Having all the right answers to life's situation is very good
but reality check number one.
Not to discourage you from doing as you should,
since life is easier said than done.
Have you the discipline?
And do you have what it takes to make those words reality?
Do you get sidetracked?
Lose focus with mistakes or get discouraged by human frailty?

To Be True to You

What would make me such a good friend,
a friend who is true to you?
What can I do to let you see that you have high value to me?
Where can I take you to show you how special you are and why?
To comfort you and lift your spirits high
If there was a key to the most special place in my heart
If there was a word, the meaning of only you and I knew
If I could make a special wish in your mind come true
If there were a jewel so big, so priceless,
times by hundred and it's you
The special things I wish you could see, would tell on me
The special thoughts I wish you could hear, bring me that smile
The special words that I wish you understood so you could see
The special expression on my face would let you know that I like
your style

Still-Small Voice

In a still-small voice you speak to me
Through the rain and the thunder
I can find serenity
When I open my heart
And just let you speak in love
You meet with me in a quiet place
To feel your Spirit and Grace
Where I worship you
And give you all the praise

Spirituality

You believe in God, don't you?

Have you spoken to him?

You'd be surprised what talking can do

Try talking to him one day; just say, "Hello, Lord, hi"; it will feel silly

Say it in your heart; just give it a try, though you feel silly

Sheep

A wolf in sheep's clothing, yeah right!
Your bark is worse than your bite.
Faux pas wolf, full of vim and fight
Confrontation! Full of fear and fright
Sheep and wolf night and day
Erroneous as seeing without sight
Sheep in wolf's clothes
Sheep? Wolf? Who knows!

On Life

Such cliché remarks as life isn't fair or words are just air.
They seem not to be thought out, why and what were they said about?
Your life is what you make it, so try to make the best of it.
You should not do what others expect you to do,
do what is right for you.
Be yourself, live your life to your expectations,
not other people's limitations.
If you love, love with all your heart; if you give in part,
you receive in part.
Don't be afraid to go after what you want; if you don't, then you
can't.
Have faith in what you do and others will have faith in you.

Every Day

I see my Bible every day; I don't read it, I don't want to pray.
My mind is troubled with obstacles in my way.
But all that has to change as I learn to deal with them.

On Love

I believe in it, but God more than it
I can give it in un-parallel amount
But less in giving, I like to receive it
I hang on to the little things, they count
What is life without it? Nonexistent!
Love and need of it make the world go 'round
Most people fear it, but they should embrace un-reluctant
Embrace it for its good and bad; let it abound

Food

Don't let food bring an end to you and me
Because it's not that important
Though it is not fair that you give up something
I too will sacrifice my dietary content
We will not be greedy, abstain from all food
That is unhealthy and exercise regularly.
Taking time to care for our bodies the right way
And as a family we're doing something good
For each other and it will bring us closer
It is good to begin healthier living and loving each other longer
By sacrificing all unhealthy food.

You

So I was thinking about you
Maybe you were thinking of me too
See, I know things are different now
Because we're much farther apart, and how?
Well because of distractions and such
The crazy things in my way, it's so much
So I cleared my mind and heart for you
Because I need you and I really miss you too
Be patient with me as we get back together
This roller-coaster relationship is something I treasure
So here we go one step at a time
I just have to say also that I'm glad you are mine

Welcome to Maranatha

"Welcome" it is a word with a lot of wonderful charms
And I want to say we welcome you here with open arms
What does this word mean; how can I make you happy
To me it says I'm glad to see you, I appreciate your company
I hope you stay all day, so relax, enjoy the sermon
And when it's all over, shake hands with the person
And if you don't mind, a friendly hug and smile
Then please stay and worship with us a while
Open your heart and be receptive to God's Holy Word
We want you to have a blessed day to meditate on what you heard
So when church is over, you will leave here lifted
And next week come back again to be filled with the Spirit
And to our members, who make Maranatha a special place,
Let our guests see God's love in your heart, shining out on your face
And remember Maranatha; its meaning always the same
Maranatha Jesus is coming again

Musings from the Edge of My Comfort Zone: Where Life Begins?

An Essay

I sat there in his car in the back of my mind;
I knew it was going to take place
But I was so taken by the present that I closed it out of my mind.
In awe just by being close, I lost my mind.
We went for a brief ride in some ·
Seemingly familiar territory, but this place was new to me.
He opened the door and let me inside. I watched him lock the door
And come close. I looked everywhere but in his eyes.
Suddenly he pulled me into him somewhat, catching me off guard
I looked at him; we looked at each other
as he gently stole a kiss from my lips.
That all-too-familiar feeling came over me,
from the pit of my stomach
Rising, reaching, and tightening in my chest.
I took a deep breath and kissed him
As softly as I could, then with each intensifying waves of emotion I
kissed him more,
But adding a sweet get addictive passion to it,
his knees buckled at that moment he held his lips. And I
realized I had power.
His eyes tighter, as he smiled, he took my hands and placed them
on his chest and moving them slowly
down his stomach, down, stopping slowly at the generous priapism
that I felt rising steadily between us...

I Dare to Bare

I dare to bare myself to the world
To let them see the inside of me and let them share a part of my heart
But that task is too great, too much at stake
I can't let anyone in lest they know my sin
Yes, I have a love, yes, a very true love
He knows me well, but he will never tell
Because we dare to bare our hearts to each other

Live a Little

Live a little, love for me, I can't
I had my son at twenty-three
Live a little means being free
To come and go, stay or leave
Live a little, love for me, I can't
Live a little makes me feel guilty
Because that's what I'd be doing if I didn't have him
I would live at the gym
I would ride my motorcycle every day

Big Dreamer

You know Joseph was a big dreamer, and God blessed him to be in charge of another man's country. I want to dream big all the time, and people, when you want a dream, you hang around people who dream big also. My dreams are to become financially free and quit working for the man. I want to work only because I feel like it, not because I have to. My dreams include my son's tuition being paid for the rest of his life, and his schooling. My dreams include my son working only because he feels like it and not because he has to. I dream of being a homeowner and owning multiple properties, and not depending on a man to support my family. I dream of being able to tell my future husband, "Baby, let's not go into work today. Let's just stay in and enjoy each other's company or let's go travel somewhere today." I dream of giving him a surprise on any given day for any given reason and not have money be an issue. Finances and the lack of management is a big factor in many of the divorces in this country. I dream of who I'm going to marry; I already know who he is. I dream of being financially free before I get married, and when I get married I will tell my boo, "Babe, you can go to work if you want to, but I am chilling at the house today." I know that persistence and consistency will cause you to reap the fruits of your labor. I know that I am officially a big dreamer.

Love, Debbie

What Is Success? (A Journal Entry)

On Tuesday, 29 January, I asked our intern (I will call him Dr. Don), "What is success?" I expected a brilliant answer since he is a doctor. Brilliant or not, I will let you decide. He said, "What is success? Success is maximizing your potential." He also stated that no one has the same potential. I think his answer was accurate. No one knows another man's potential, but each person knows his or her own potential. This brings me to the next point, a question. Who, or by what standards, do we have our success? If only I know my potential, then my success is relative to me. But my preconceived notions of success had to come from somewhere, right? Well, they did. They are learned or observed. Society teaches me what success should look like. For example, for your degree, lawyers, doctors, or any job that allows you to bring in a substantial amount of money or allows for some prestige is considered success or successful. In my opinion, success also has a lot to do with material things required, which allow for a successful perception. But it is, as the good doctor stated, success is maximizing your potential, but I want to go even further and say it is maximizing your individual potential.

This Place

There is a place,
I want to be there
There is where my heart always smiles
I am always happy in this place and
I'm alone, no end in sight for miles.
In this place, there are evergreen trees
Everywhere tall, majestic, and beautiful
And in these trees are birds singing a
Beautiful melody for me, lovely and cheerful
The grass is green and soft
The flowers in the garden are bright, colorful, and scented.
The air is crisp and fresh, each beast is
Full of life and energy as God intended.
I can think in this place, it is so quiet
And peaceful, I am the queen of my life.
I am never upset or sad there, never worried or angry
Never at war, never in strife.
Is here even such a place?
How much do I have to pay?
And how would I even get in?
There is such a place in my heart
And better yet in heaven.

I Pay

I'm paying high price for all my carnal nights, and I pay this price for the rest of my life.

Given

My love, you may not realize it, but I am given to you
We became one in two thousand that first night
when I gave myself to you
You knew me and I you, and we have been knowing each other
since
You are my husband and I am your
Wife in a Spiritual sense
A man could only know a woman if she was his wife

My Love Song

Bubbling laughter from a happy little boy
Dancing eyes and shining smile fill my heart with joy
The soft, caring voice of the man in my life
Tender eyes and comforting smile, I should be his wife
A soft kiss from tiny little lips
With every beat, my proud heart skips
An emotion-filled hug that says I know
You have to go, though I don't want you to
I'll be there for you, you know
I'm full and content with these two
Men, they are my family, my gift from heaven

Love Letters in the Sand

While walking by a tent this morning
I looked down in the sand
It look different from the
Hard, rock-filled, heavily trodden stuff covering this land
It was soft and rippled,
It reminded me of that beach, you know the one
Then a thought came to mind
Why not write "I love you" So I looked around for something to
Write with, preferably a stick
Because I did not want to ruin the sand
By stepping in it
I found something; it was perfect!
I trace the letters of the words that they spelled
Then took a picture of them
Because of how I felt,
Happy and proud to express my love for you
And a little rebellious too
It had not been done before
It was a first and I did it
Because of how I felt about you

Jovan

I guess I just want to love you
I guess I want you to be happy
I guess I want to share me with you
I guess I want you to love me
Supposedly I think about you a lot
Supposedly I even care
But even if I did, so what?
It means nothing when you're not here
It's probably true what they say
Absence makes the heart grow fonder
Maybe I want you more every day
The way you are, well, it's no wonder

Jhordan Kimball Walters "Pooh"

When I look at my son, this is what I see
A beautiful, soft angel with funny faces like me
A precious little body of calm and contentment
I fell in love with him and fall deeper each moment
He puts a smile on my face
Evertime I see him, I just go with the ride that will never grow dim
Love, Mom

The Loveless

I loved the softness of his lips, the wanting in his kiss
The rough grazing of his stubble face against mine
His face, his hand felt almost like silk, but he seemed so loveless.
My head on his chest when he slept reminded me of back
When I was a little one lying in the crook of my daddy's arm
With my head on his chest, my daddy's heartbeat was strong.
Loud, mine and Daddy's would eventually feel like one beat
But I could hardly hear his heartbeat; he seemed so hard and loveless.
When distance, the sea, and sand kept us apart
I felt connected and close to you because we talked.
Hearing from you put me on top of the world
You helped my heart and soul to smile and breathe easy.
But when you came home, you didn't even call me
You left me out for what seemed like forever and I missed you.
But I got over it, the physical distance closed between us
But the connection was weak and I missed you.
I kept in touch, but you would never text back.
I have been proud of you the whole time I have known you
To me you seemed exceptional; I wanted you to be proud of me too
But I really had nothing to show for it except feeling like a loser.
More than anything I loved your support, your wisdom, and advice,
whatever you had to offer.
You are on the fast track, leaving me in the dust.
In your wake I couldn't even try to tell you how I felt
Because all the good things in your life caused you to forget
The little people like me.
Loveless was you trying to put me on display

like an object to your friends

I don't mind showing myself off for you alone, but in public?
Well, I just felt cheap; asking me to turn around so you can see
made me feel cheap.

A f*** is what you do with the chick you meet at the club; spending
quality time is exclusive.

It seems you may be the father figure I've wanted to connect with
since the distance took me away from my father when I was twelve.

Been fighting this ever since; you are about as hairy as he was; your
face stubble reminded me of him.

I hated him for cheating on my mother and treating her like trash.

I wanted to love you, but I can't do it the way you want it.

If you didn't have two pennies to rub together, I would love you.

The Eyes of My Angel

In the eyes of my angel, I find release
When this cold, hard world gives me no peace
When my angel is near me, I forget my cares
Wrapped in your arms without worries or fears
In the eyes of my angel I have contentment
He fills my mind, my heart with warm sentiment
My angel is my love; he knows and understands me
When I look in my angel's eyes, they set me free

The Heart of a Lover

Burnt by the cold
Evergreen grow old
Atlantis is found
Very unlikely these to be
Endurance of time and love, you see
Never will I let go of thee
Purest of them all
Let no harm befall
Outpour your love on me
Caress my heart with all that is lovely
Hear not the plea of another
Everlasting be the heart of a lover
Temporary are our loss of words
For in the silence our hearts are heard
Deep and deeper still will this stream run
Till earth herself is then undone
Once lonesome hearts now twined as one
Stronger, stronger with the rise of every sun

Seclusion

That's the name of the game
Lackluster and without fame
The bigger the wall
The harder it falls
No one in, everyone out
I need seclusion, no doubt

Outskirts

She said, "Tell him the sun and moon rise in his eyes."
Her universe is small. She has only one son,
You, her new and rising moon,
And a small cluster of stars, large, brilliant stars.
In their romantic solar system
Their gravitational pull to each other was intense.
As they got closer, it seems that their rotational orbit increased.
The centrifugal effects have separated them.
Their Sun and Moon once danced with each other,
Now they are flung to the far reaches of the galaxy.
The only thing keeping her in the orbit of his solar system is an
agape love;
She teeters somewhere on the outskirts.

Again

A final breath or a last sigh of relief
My heart is sad, but I will see you again!
A distant stare or a longing gaze
You long for a better place, where I will see you again
You spoke of heaven often, Jesus' handmaid of dust
You have taken leave of this place, but I will see you again
We saw what sin has done, whittled away from what once was
You will be better than ever when I see you again
Your beautiful smile will be more radiant than I remember
With your head on Christ's bosom when I see you again
Tirelessly you worked for Jesus, and now He gives you rest
When you open your eyes, you will see Jesus…again!

Paper Aero Plane

He's fascinated with aero planes, especially the paper kind.
He believes that he could make the best one if only in his mind.
But every attempt he made to fly one was an attempt he failed.
But he improved his technique and he has prevailed.

That's Some Audacity

To think you deserve to love me
Love me why? Love me how?
Love me from eternity to now
You have made up your mind
For a future undecided
Are we clandestine?
Or simpleminded
From this moment
Your love shall be my content

Illusions

Illusions of grandeur all in my head
Just because of this man lying here in my bed
This night in September my heart was broken
Reality paid me a visit, and this is the token
My eternal optimism had done it again
With crazy ideas thought of by the emotionally insane
You can fool some of them some of the time, you see
But you can't fool all of them all of the time
So I managed to fool myself thinking of love
Promising my heart to you, my gift from above
Adding things that weren't there
Hoping you'd add up or even come near
When will I see this is not my job to do?
 Lord, changing people is reserved for you
Time does heal all wounds, but time is too slow in my greatest need
So anger and hatred can take its place but still can't beat
I'm in the healing race, angry and betrayed
Always short in living time with always when you are forgiven

You Conquered Me

I am a woman in search of love, warmth, and safety.
I was a tower of strength and pride.
I was your conquest, your Mount Everest,
and you set out to dominate me.
I was no challenge for you. I didn't put up a fight.
I didn't need to struggle.
I wanted you, but why should you have to work to get me?
I made it easy.
I am a troubled woman, my mind set on equal.
I too had one last conquest.
I wanted you. You were perfect in my eyes,
to be my husband, to be my lover.
You were perfect to be my son's father figure and mentor;
you were perfect.
I thought if I made easy I would save time.
But that backfired, because time is all you take.
I was happy with loving you,
but you were not satisfied with me. I was not a challenge.
You never claimed me as your own.
You never asked me to be yours. You did not want me.
But you cannot have my joy, my peace,
my dignity, my laughter, my essence.
I will not give you any more.
I am at peace with my beauty, inside and out.
I will not be conquered by you.

A Fight

From where I sit and peer into my future,
not very much seems to be clear
Today I see a road heading toward the horizon,
but the sun is going down.
At first I see myself only,
sometimes someone else flickers in and out, here and there
 His image becomes steady with me;
we are holding hands, my salt-and-pepper locks windblown
As we walk, we laugh and talk like sweethearts,
we stop and look at each other and embrace.
He has no hair left on his head;
he has innocent eyes that see just the best things in me
He lovingly runs his fingers through my hair;
his hands draw me in as he kisses my face.
He tells me it's been a long journey to get here,
but he made it and he is happy I waited
He was sincere,
he said he wanted to spend the rest of his life making things right.
My reality is as uncertain as my future,
I want to smile but I am very frustrated
I love you, I am worth it,
and you can't just give up and let me go without a fight.

Musings over Thirty

Feeling Myself

What do I do when I am feeling myself? I write about it. I have over fifteen years of journals in a trunk at the foot of my bed. Maybe one day my son will read them and have them published. I think that is actually my dying wish, that he would publish my life story. My life story is not a fabulous one. I am not famous. I am not an intellect, but I am intelligent. I have a plethora of insecurities, and I fight with myself daily to overcome them. There are days when I feel like everyone hates me or that I am just not good enough, that I am stupid and worthless. There are days when I think that everyone thinks I am retarded. These thoughts just depress me even further, and it's even worse when I think, about the boyfriend, fiancé, husband I don't have but want so desperately. I ask myself and God, "What the hell is wrong with me?" and why do I run up on men who only want to hurt me, when all I want to do is love them? Why do they rape me or sexually harass me? Why do they lie to me? Why do they cheat on me? And why do I let the "seemingly" good ones go? I have let my life pass me by romantically in an attempt to spare my heart, but it has only been broken time and again.

At least once per month, I get depressed and emotional. I have monitored my cycle, and honestly, my emotional rise and fall is random. Sometimes it's before or after, sometimes during; there really is no rhyme or reason. But during those times when I am feeling myself, I feel like I have a certain clarity, yet it is not clarity. I feel vulnerable, like I want to be held or just bury my face in the hairy chest of the boyfriend (this month I am in love with Arjun Kapoor's hairy chest) I don't have and cry. And that is the point where I don't want him to say anything, just hold me and let me let it out. Let me explain that I am emotional, and I know I am being very irrational, but I still need to let it out...to release it. And all he has to do is make me feel safe and feel like it's okay. Today is that day for me.

Feeling You

Right now, I think you are selfish, and I hate you. Why do you daily accept that I love you and daily accept my support of you? But you know you don't love me, you know you know you cannot, yet you try to keep me on your team. What about me? What about my heart? Why can't you just say, "I know you love me, but I cannot reciprocate, and I cannot ask you to keep loving me like the way you do?"

I Don't Like It

My friend—at least I thought he was—we trained together and were comrades in arms. I was naïve to the plot as it thickened while my back was turned. I was a damsel in distress; I learned that military lodging would not pay for my hotel until the dates listed on my orders, and I was two days early with no place to stay and very little money to afford it either. Tired and jetlagged, due to my long flight in to Virginia from Italy, and ready to take the path of least resistance, not thinking anything bad could happen to me, I agreed to stay with my friend when he offered me his room. I was grateful, and I was relieved to take a shower, change, and jump into bed. My friend had left me alone for a few hours so I could get settled, but when he returned and saw me in bed, he protested and begged me to go out with him and another friend. Reluctantly, I went out with them, despite my better judgment telling me to stay in and sleep. Dressed in my drab gray-brown mini-dress with matching leggings and brown flats, my medium-length hair done in a whimsically romantic side braid, with sparkling chandelier earrings, the ensemble had me raking in the ego-boosting compliments. But we went to a local bar with another friend. They say not everyone who calls you a friend intends to do good to you. We drank! Brown drinks, blue drinks, honey-colored drinks, and beer! I knew nothing of drinking, nothing about eating prior to drinking, nothing about drinking slowly. I knew nothing! And after a time, the room moved in a surreal slow motion, my head turned and it took seconds for the rest of the room to catch up. And when I stood up to walk the floor moved away from me, I am sure I was hilarious to look at. Before long we left the bar, since nothing was happening there, and I was such a sloppy drunk, I had to be carried to the car. We arrived back at the hotel and he was such a gentleman. He helped walk as I would have probably face-planted into the asphalt had he not. After we made it to his room, he helped me to my bed, took off my shoes, and tucked me in. I was almost asleep until I had to use the bathroom. He acted like a friend, and he helped me to the bathroom, since I could not make it there on my own. He brought me back and I collapsed on his bed, since it was closer to the bathroom than mine, but it was all convenient for us both. My head was spinning, thoughts flitting in and out, like a thousand butterflies in a meadow filled with flowers, and me trying to catch one with a butterfly net. Once I caught one, it would escape; my incoherence was my doom. He tucked me in on the side closest to the bathroom and jumped in on the other side; we talked and laughed about nothing. But he asked to kiss me, and that was okay, but then he wanted more and I was useless to stop him physically, but was he really thinking about that? He tried to penetrate, but I said, "No, I don't want to." He persisted, and I insisted, no. He asked why. But I just didn't want to. He begged to please me, but I could not say yes. He pulled out and decided to use his mouth, and I became upset. I begged him not to. "No, I don't like it!" Finally he stopped. It seemed like forever, but it really was not that long. I rolled onto my side to face the wall. I was disgusted, mostly with myself for making all the bad choices that led to that moment. Now what was I to do?

Learning Happiness

In the wake of yet another breakup, I find that I am getting more and more numb to this kind of thing. Basically realizing that stuff happens, people change, and relationships end. I just remember the good times, but I know I struggle not to slip into my default mode of being bitter and angry. It's hard not to do it. I feel vindictive at times. But I also feel content at times. I am looking forward to the time in the near future when I am always content. I feel as though it is just right there. I am letting go. I am tired of being my own emotional prisoner. As the great Bob Marley stated, "Emancipate yourself from mental slavery; none but ourselves can free our mind."

Your mind is more powerful than you may realize.

Assume the role of a successful person and make it obvious to yourself and others, and your brain will follow. There are no guarantees in the world, just vicissitudes and opportunities. Opportunities are always worth pursuing. Think of a problem as nothing more than an opportunity in work clothes.

Here's to your success! (Good Morning! I love you)

Like
Comment
Share

The Power of Prayer

If no one has figured it out yet, I will announce it. I believe in the power of prayer. Also, I most definitely believe in miracles. I may have told this story already (I am getting up in age, so I really don't remember). Well, here it goes again. Once upon a time, about a year ago, I came to Savannah, GA. I was getting a new job (yay me), and I was going to be a Platoon Leader (PL) (yes, I am in the Army). Obviously I was ecstatic at the prospect of doing great things and being a charismatic leader of troops, loved by all and feared by all too. But I also had goals of how my career should progress (I was not loved or feared by all; I was just there mostly learning and getting near- impossible tasks done by my awesome NCOs and soldiers).

I know that after I was a platoon leader, I wanted to be a Company Executive Officer (XO) (that's a big deal; I am second in command), and after that...well, let me not jump too far ahead. I began to pray for what I wanted, but I was determined, and I knew that while prayer works, fasting would definitely drive the point home. So I embarked on a forty-day fast (from unhealthy foods), not once but twice. As time progressed, it became evident that I would probably not ever get an XO position in my current organization. After about seven months, I was rated for my time as the platoon leader, and my evaluation was good. Something within me stirred, and I sent an email to my company commander requesting that the (my) PL position be given to a new lieutenant (LT) who needed PL time. At the same time that was happening, the battalion commander (BN CDR) asked the new LT what job he wanted, and he said the PL job (I see God merrily at work here). I had never met this new LT, and I had no idea about the conversation he was having with the BN CDR. But as soon as I sent the email to my company commander, the BN CDR, knew what was going on, and within seventy-two hours it was a done deal. I did have some emotional qualms (I felt like I quit my platoon and I wanted it back). I was assigned to the BN headquarters (a place that equates to hell for me). I vehemently protested that move (only to myself, my family, my boyfriend, and the new LT).

But God had something better in store (wait for it). About three weeks after the transition, we had to execute our field training exercise (FTX), which was three weeks long (SIDE BAR: My darling boyfriend, bless his heart, encouraged me to take the BN promotion despite my protests. He said, "You will do well and learn"). In the final week of the FTX, my BN XO called me and said I was nominated from our BN to interview for a job in DIVISON (all caps added for emphasis LOL). As if all the military acronyms have not already confused you, let me explain the hierarchy of the organization briefly, from the bottom to the top. The platoon is within a company, a company is within a battalion, a battalion is within a brigade, and a brigade is within a division. Also, there are several platoons on a company, several companies in a battalion, several battalions in a brigade, and several brigades on a division. So you get the picture: I got a super-duper promotion! (Paygrade remains the same, though, but organizationally speaking, let's just say I am blessed.) My BN XO said I probably wouldn't get the job because I was going up against other LTs in the brigade (thanks for the vote of confidence, sir). As the hand of God works, I got selected above all the other LTs in my brigade (thank you, Lord). Then I got word the day prior to the end of our FTX, I was selected for the interview with my potential new commander. I was sent out of the field a day early. I bought a new uniform and new boots, and I prayed. I had no idea what to expect, and I was not given any information except that it was for a company XO position.

I prayed on the way to the interview. I called and asked my friends to pray, and I posted on Facebook that I needed prayers. My new (soon-to-be) boss called me into his office, and I shook hands and sat and we just had a chat. I was myself, confident, well articulated, and honest with my answers, and he liked what he got. I think what won him over was the fact that I am almost as old as he is, yet I am willing to learn from someone who is younger than I am. My contact information was recorded after the interview, and I left with the knowledge and confidence that I had the job.

But after two weeks, I had not heard any information. I had not even received orders taking me to my new position. So I sent an email to let them know I was still alive and very much interested in the job. And I waited, slightly embarrassed, as I was expecting to leave my BN very quickly, but by now, it had been close to a month since the interview. So I started another forty-day fast, and I told God exactly what I wanted, and I said, "You have opened up these doors for me, and I know you have not shut them, but I am still letting you know that I am claiming it and I want it." Well, he answered my prayers!

After close of business, as I was out to dinner with a friend, I got a call from my NEW BOSS! He said he wanted me to start as soon as possible and put me in contact with my new company commander (doing the happy dance!!).

I leave you with this final thought: It's not what you know but who you know. For me, I know God, and it seems that knowing Him trumps everything else.

P.S.: This is not the first time that God has done something like this for me :)

Cowardice

We are not cherished; we have been abused and torn down by our previous relationships gone wrong. I find it hard to look at any man in a trusting way. They hurt you, whether they mean to or not. They say anything to arouse trust and love, and when you decide to love them in every sense of the word, they say things like, "I don't know what love is" or "I have no intention of loving anyone." If this is so, then why did you look at me and decide I was worth you lying to?

If you don't intend to love, then don't awaken love in another.

It Takes a Strong Heart to Love

Love. I can say one thing for sure, There is a lot to be said on the topic. But the only love advice I think worth following and is most difficult to follow is from God.

God's love for us is everlasting. That's what I believe. It's unconditional—that's what I know.

It is without conditions; you get it and you don't have to reciprocate. You get it and that's that.

That kind of love changes hearts and people. That kind of love is the greatest love, but no one seems to realize that.

That kind of love is the kind I hope for and the kind I want to give. Not just to a lover but to everyone.

In relationships, that's the kind of love that lasting relationships are built on. But they also include respect, compromise, trust, and care.

I am waiting for that.

Something Beautiful

I wanted to fill and rearrange the space immediately, but I couldn't. As with anything in life, at least any relationship that has run its course, you have to respect the space, honor it, honor the spirit and essence of what was. Clean the space, then gradually transform that space into something spiritual and beautiful.

The Wish

For you to feel something, you are being consumed, eaten alive by your desire. It's as though you want me to stand witness to your self-destruction. I love you. But I want you to love me too. Not take advantage of the fact that I care for you. My pride and ego are so hurt to be rejected by you...to be shoveled off to the friend zone. To me this means you have someone new.

Shooting Star

You are my shooting star, flying across my night sky
I would try to hold on to as long as I can, I make a wish
You are on a set path, with no deviation
You came in as fast as you left, bright, dazzling, stupendous
You have left me in your wake,
All I have left of you is the remnant of your tail.

The Last Hope

I want to be held, and I want kisses on my forehead. To have the fact that I am a woman, validated, meaning...nothing. It doesn't matter. I am afraid to tell you anything, because you are unfeeling at this time. It would mean nothing to you. You would only see it from the perspective of a window shopper, looking at something nice, that you could see yourself having, but no actual intention of buying. You were the last hope I had. Before you, I never intended to love, and now this has passed its expiration date. I am again without. You awakened love within me, and yet you had no actual intention of loving me. Was this a sick joke? Does it bring you pleasure?

Understanding from My Limited Perspective

Having the perspective of your partner (objective or subjective) provides an angle you have never seen before. Now, what you choose to do with it is a different story. Let me say a few short words (as if there is such a thing with me) on understanding, that is, in a relationship. To say it is important is a just stating the obvious. The depth of understanding needed goes a lot deeper than we may realize.

Understanding yourself is a start, as I see it. I had to learn and understand why I behave the way I do in relationships. I realized that if I did not understand why, I could not fix my behavior. That took trial and error, and a crap ton of apologies, which made me humble. Understanding the nature of your relationship is also, in my opinion, a necessity. Both you and your partner need to have a discussion on that. It may be difficult, but it's better than assuming you have something you really don't. Understand that certain relationships MUST progress much more slowly than others. Long-distance relationships are difficult. Throw in a huge culture difference in the mix and two completely different personalities, and you have the perfect recipe for a "soup sandwich."

In order to gain understanding about yourself, introspect is imperative. You have to sit with yourself and analyze your root cause, your trigger for certain behaviors, and you must put in the work to address or fix it. Changing is not easy, but it is necessary. In my relationships, I needed to learn to be calm, I had anxieties about everything, and I was like a nervous kid with allergies to everything... including breathing. And I did entirely too much (but that is true for everything...my nickname is "team too much").

Even now, it is difficult to not have a million things, two blogs, a book of poems, a family, a partner, a new job that will demand more than the others did, Toastmasters, new moneymaking endeavors, and aggressively managing my career and higher education (masters, dual major). So, you see, it is easy to become a jack of all trades and a master of none. Side bar: I have ADHD.

Eventually, something is going to fall through the cracks.

My final point on understanding, you must understand your partner. Definitely easier said than done (especially when you are not even on the same continent). But it is not impossible, and I definitely believe patience, a level of commitment to being together, maturity, and the ability to communicate openly are needed.

What Would You Do If You Were Not Afraid?

The question of the day for me is: What would you do if you were not afraid? Yesterday I met with some young ladies from my battalion for a lunch and learn session. We talked about change, why it is difficult for so many of us, and techniques to overcome those difficulties. We covered theories from books like *Who Moved My Cheese?* and *Switch* (both books that I absolutely adore). However, the question that struck me (strange that it never did before, since I read the book already) was the question written on a wall in a maze by an indecisive man (mouse) called "Haw" (*Who Moved My Cheese?*): What would you do if you were not afraid? Ladies and gentlemen, I submit to you today that the mind is the prison that holds you captive, and fear is the key used to lock the doors. I have read in the Bible that "perfect love casts out fear" (1 John 4:18). I believe this is entirely and unequivocally true. Not just in the case of romantic love, but unconditional love (even for strangers). We can most definitely attempt to cultivate love for all; however, I will be the first to admit that this is a MOST difficult task (especially with antagonists, who persist in pushing my buttons...that is another story). But with those persons, they are the perfect ones to practice love on (I curse myself for saying that...because I would rather throat punch them than be loving :( ).

My challenge to you today is this: Every morning when you wake up, just after you pray (thanking God for waking you up), once your feet touch the ground, ask yourself, "Self, what would you do if you were not afraid?" Take a moment to think about it, then write it down. For me, the question would apply in small doses. By that I mean think about what I would do today if I were not afraid.

I would tell Captain Man that everyone already knows he does not know all the answers, even though he pretends to. I would think of a new way to motivate my soldiers to take positive steps to self-improvement. I would volunteer for the toughest assignment that no one wants! I would slay it! Because you can never go wrong if no one has done it before you :) (Tip of the day...if you want to be a superstar in your organization). So tell me, what would you do if you were not afraid?

Today, I Caught Myself Asking, "Where is God in All of This?"

It's not a question of existence; for me it never was, never is, nor will it ever be. It's a question of what place or priority have I given him. In all my endeavors for success and being the all-around queen of awesome, where did I place Him? I observed here in India every home and business place has a shrine or mini-temple of worship. Every day almost everyone goes through the twenty-one or twenty-two steps for puja (prayer).

My worship of God is my own, because I understand that it is my personal relationship with Him that has to be developed and solid. I do admire the way Muslim and Hindu believers worship...it is serious for them, like a heart attack, compulsory, no questions asked. It's a must and I love that. Business and daily life do not start until puja is complete. On Fridays, business is closed and Muslim believers go to temple for prayer.

It makes me question my priority of my Heavenly Father and realize that I am taking Him for granted in the way I worship...or at least my lack thereof.

Rejecting religion based on the way I was raised:

I was raised in a very conservative Christian home. Jewelry was not permitted, and what you said and did were always being scrutinized by others. My religion taught that all other religions were wrong. I never questioned that belief until recently, because that is how I was raised.

Rejecting the theory that my life is harder because I am black.

Today I had a discussion with my boyfriend about begin black and being an officer in the army. I had just completed my duty day, and I called my boyfriend to let him know that I was walking to his workplace. I got there and the car was locked, so I tried calling and his phone was busy, so I sent a text. I realized I had homework due so I sat on his car trunk, took out my iPad and textbook, and started taking notes. He came out and yelled at me, saying it was tacky for me to sit on the trunk of his car. At first I thought he was kidding, so I asked and he said he was serious.

So I opened a discussion because I was confused. He said I looked tacky and undisciplined, especially because I was in uniform. He said I am a black female and an officer and there are people who do not want me around. He said it is a struggle and people would perceive me as ghetto.

I promptly stated I was raised differently. Children don't notice skin color until they are taught to differentiate. I stated that all people struggle, white people, black, Asian, and so forth, so what makes me any different? I earned my commission just like everyone else who is an officer. Anything worth having and keeping is worth working/struggling for. So I never expected being an officer to be any different.

As for people who perceive me as ghetto, they are entitled to their thoughts. They are ignorant in my eyes because they did not take the time to find out why I was sitting on the car or what I was doing (homework). As for people who don't want me here (as an officer), that does not bother me. They have the problem because I am already here, and they will have to figure out how they planned to process that fact.

I simply refuse to let my skin color be my hang-up, at work or anywhere else.

My boyfriend told me that when he went to France on a weekend trip, two females grabbed their purses when they saw him, he took offense to it. So I asked why he thought they did it. Someone gave them a reason to feel and act that way. They are ignorant because they don't know you personally but if they did they would never have done it. I told him to forgive their ignorance, and not hold it against them.

This Is Life

In 2012 I was introduced to the work of David Foster Wallace. I had not heard of him prior to that. I listened to an excerpt from his commencement speech to the 2005 graduating class of Kenton College. His speech, entitled "This Is Water," addressed the immense and fascinating power of choice. We are the masters of what we choose to think about; obviously we are used the default way of thinking, which is very self-absorbed, narcissistic, and egotistical. Often we fail to realize that there is a universe of which we are not the brightest star, the largest sun, nor are we the center of said universe (ouch, that does hurt a little). Mr. Wallace started his speech with an anecdote about two young fish swimming merrily by in a fish bowl, when there passed by an older fish swimming in the opposite direction, who said to both the younger fish, "How's the water, boys?" The two young fish looked at each other in confusion and asked, "What the heck is water?"

The idea of teaching one to think or to choose what to think about and to rewire their default setting the focal point of David Foster Wallace's speech. One is considered well adjusted once able to rewire their default way of thinking. Paying attention to the here and now is most difficult when your mind is loudest thing you hear. David states that the mind is a great servant but a terrible master, which is probably why most suicides committed with firearms shoot themselves in the head; they want to kill the terrible master.

How do we prevent ourselves from living our lives as walking dead, slaves to our default setting? How do we keep ourselves from falling into "boredom, routine, and petty frustration"? I submit to you as David Foster Wallace did, that we CHOOSE TO THINK. We must be selective in our choice of thought (mind-blowing concept). As opposed to thinking of yourself as the victim or the inconvenienced, take the time to consider others. Consider that someone's situation is worse off than yours, and your concerns are the least of the worries in the world.

Once we have truly mastered how to think, how to pay attention, our eyes will be opened to the belief that we have other options. It is now within our power to experience a "crowded, hot, slow, consumer hell type of situation as not only meaningful but sacred, on fire with the same force that lit the stars; Love, fellowship," etc. We get to decide how we will see the situations; we decide what has meaning and what does not.

Freedom, the truly important kind, entertains discipline, attention, and awareness, the ability to indubitably care about others and to make repetitious sacrifices for them every day in ways that garner no recognition or praise. The alternative is our default setting, the rat race, the numbness of rote rehearsal and routine.

I leave you with this final thought:

Life before death, awareness, to stay conscious and alive is extremely difficult to do, and we literally have to remind ourselves daily, "This is water, this is water, this is water" (THIS IS LIFE).

She Left Me Today

She left me today, even though I knew it was coming.
I didn't think on it, nor did I think much of it.
But she is gone, she left with, grace and beauty, and poise.
She filled a beautiful space in my heart,
one I never thought could be occupied.
She grew on me, and I grew to love her.
But she left me today, peacefully
She promised to return soon, but I know it's temporary
I created a space for her,
I wanted her to leave me better than when she came
And I actually feel she did;
she deals with hurt and pain better than I do
And there are days when I certainly wish I were as innocent as she
I am left with that empty space that she once filled.
What am I to do with it? I can celebrate her, reflect.
Reflect on the essence she left, and the lessons
She left traces behind, I would call it shedding of her old skin
Evidence of her growth and evolution.
She certainly is not the girl she was when she came here
She is an independent, free spirit with a big and beautiful soul
At times I can't help but to think I have done her wrong,
I know I did
Most times inadvertently but failed to think she has outgrown me
I love her, but her season has come and gone,
and it is time for her to move on.
I miss her, I am lonely when I had her,

and I did not think much of her presence
I was glad she was there, but I didn't acknowledge her much.
We spoke, we laughed and did things together
I told her how I felt, I told her from my heart, honestly
And everything I gave her, she took heed of and improved
But now I am without her. And everyone else, it seems.
All the people I love so deeply are miles away from me
And I have no one to comfort me, to lift me up.
I certainly don't want to burden anyone with my woes
Because they have woes of their own to bear
But there is no one I trust that I can lean on here.

Musings to India, with Love

Yesterday

Yesterday all my troubles seemed too far away, and now it looks as though they're to stay.... Not complaining about troubles at all. It's just that I want my post to be about yesterday, and that was the first song that popped into my head. Yesterday was nice; this guy (Ramuji Krishnamurti) hooked me up with an evening trip to the Gateway of India! The "tour" included lunch and dinner, my own personal tour guide, and taxi driver. Also, my tour guide laughed at me a lot because of my epic fails at speaking Hindi and eating like an Indian. I am left-handed to begin with, and in India as well as Middle Eastern countries, you DO NOT use your left hand to eat or offer/receive things from people. Why? Because the left hand is used for doing "unclean" business. So picture me attempting to break apart and eat garlic naan with my right hand. And my question of "Where are we going?" was all wrong..."kaha raho hai" and the only phrase I say fluently in Hindi is "nahin hai," which comes in handy for just about everything!

The Gateway of India was built to commemorate King George and Queen Mary's visit in 1811 (I think). I found it interesting in at least two ways; the structure, which was commissioned by British architect George Whittet (I think), was built by Indians (obviously, since India was under British rule at the time). Also, the Gateway was the official point of exit for England when India was given back her independence, even though it was not the route they used to enter India in the first place.

Many of the cathedrals in Goa have similar construction patterns of their archways, indicative of the time period and European influence. Goa was occupied by the Portuguese, which is why there are so many Catholic churches there. I will go back today and see some more of historical Bombay, and I will take pictures (yippee!).

Happy New Year!

Journey to India

I have been sent on a journey to India, to discover the culture, people, the colors, the fragrances, the textures, tastes, and flavors that are captured within. To embody it all within myself and carry it to the rest of the world.

So far, my favorite thing about India is its spirituality. So many people have traveled there to find themselves, rejuvenate, and gain new spirituality. I'm not looking to do anything different; I just want to experience it for myself. I've fallen in love with the vitality of the culture people and the fact that everything is like a celebration.

Some of my favorite foods are from India, including curried goat, curry chicken, cabbage, white rice, and garbanzo beans, just to name a few. I like some Indian men; some of them are easy on the eyes. However, many of them are too thin for me. I realize that there is prejudice among Indians and dark people. "Indians do not necessarily like dark-skinned people; even in their own culture they do not like darker-complexion women." I do not know how true that is, but I intend to discover firsthand. Right now, what I know of India is what I've seen Bollywood movies or Indian cinema. That knowledge is biased; not all parts of India are like that, not everyone breaks into song and dance when we are happy, sad, in love, angry, lonely, or feeling cheeky. However, my goal, my intent, is to discover truth and learn about India and Indians.

At this point, I have made plans with a travel agency; my next step is to pay for the actual tour. Then, get a travel visa to India and finally pay for my ticket. While there, I want to see, feel, touch, and taste everything the culture has to offer.

Later in life, perhaps when I become a captain, I would like to adopt a little Indian girl, as well as an older Indian boy for Jhordan to play with or have for a companion.

Journey to India (Part Doh)

My life is changing before my eyes, and it's so damned exciting! In December of 2013, my therapist asked me if I was balanced. I said, "Yes, I think so." He gave me a personal survey, and I took it. Apparently I felt balanced in every area except that of relationships with the opposite sex. Well, since I had been raped in 2012 and sexually harassed in 2013, I had good reason to be unbalanced in this area. So I decided to start online dating, since it was "safe." By "safe," I mean I did not actually have to meet them in person. I got on to several dating sites, and the one I expected the least success with was the one I struck gold with.

Desi Crush.com. There I met the handsomely persistent Ramuji Krishnamurti. He is a man with a head on his shoulders, complex, smart, and fiercely protective of family and friends. Yet he had been heartbroken, and that was his burden, he longed for love, never again did he want to be betrayed because he was not rich enough. I tried to explain that having riches is not all that matters, but in his culture, success among other things is measured by how financially stable your family is. He lost the love of his life because of financial hardships his family suffered. Now, here I am, trying desperately to understand his culture, and failing miserably at it. He threw himself head on into his career, and decided to take me along as a witness to his journey. But from my perspective, he is killing himself at a much faster pace than normal, and he will never be able to enjoy the fruits of his labor.

Ramju Krishnamurti

Rivers run free, calm and placid, reflective in some places. In others rushing wildly, thrashing madly against rocks and banks, eroding nearby landscapes.

Albeit so late in my life, you brought something to my heart I was longing for. A small piece of romance, being wanted, sought after, and held in regard and esteem. You gave it to me, you validated my heart, my desire to be seen and treated as more.

Kuch nahi can

Thunderstorm

Meri Jaan, I hear the rain falling, tapping gently on my windowpane. I see the flashes of lightning ripping carelessly across the sky. The wind rustling the leaves of the trees, much the same way it rustles the skirts of ladies and girls on gusty spring day. The thunder, as it loudly cracks the atmosphere.

The drops of rain tap a soft melody in my mind; my imagination basks on a journey to you. Somewhere half the distance around the world I am locked in your embrace, and I feel the first drops of monsoon rains tapping audaciously on my face.

Tap. Tap. Tap-tap, I bury my face in your chest, your scent intoxicates me, and even if I wanted to let go I could not because I am a willing captive of yours. I hear your heartbeat. I feel it through your shirt, strong and virulent, beating deep like the tabla at a wedding celebration.

There are no words between us, just the moments etched in memory by this lingering hug. We wait, as the torrential downpour begins. You softly and convincingly kiss my face, my forehead, my cheeks, my chin, and my lips. No words, you take my hand in yours and we walk toward the direction of what feels like home.

Tuesday, February 23, 2014

Something New

To me you are something different! Ramuji Krishnamurti
You are so unexpected in every manner;
you are my first light of morning
You have placed me on a pedestal that I have known I should stand
But for some time, even I did not believe I belonged at hand
You affirm and validate me,
you restore and embolden my smile and laughter
I have endeared you to me,
hamesha meri dil mujhe maza karna, bahut shukriya!
I have always known what could and should be,
I stopped believing that is was likely
Meri Jaan, you have made the unthinkable a reality,
pardon me as I get over my anxiety.

23 March 2014

Take Your Time

Take your time, she loves you! Take your time to follow your
dreams; you know she believes in you.
Take your time to focus on being your best;
you know she is there for you.
Take your time to figure out what you want from life and love,
her love for you is unconditional.
She respects your wisdom, she supports your decisions,
and she understands your drive and passion.
She knows she cannot be first for you, she can wait.
It takes time, and right now, time is all you have.
You are a team, her success is your success,
you area her emotional pillar of strength.
Take your time, she loves you.

27 August 2014

Perfection and Completion

Seven is completion and perfection; God rested after completing creation on the seventh day.

Seven is perfection and completion; Isaac worked for Rachel's father Laban for seven years to have her hand in marriage.

Seven is perfection and completion; Laban tricked Isaac and gave him Leah, Rachel's older sister.

Seven is perfection and completion; Isaac worked another seven years for Rachel's hand in marriage, poor Leah.

Seven is perfection and completion; after seven years we enter a new cycle of life, I am leaving one, you just entered one.

Seven is perfection and completion; you are searching for more in life; you sense you are here for a purpose and you will attain it.

Seven is perfection and completion; I am in a cycle of spiritual abundance. Seven represents completion and perfection in both the physical and spiritual.

Seven is perfection and completion; there are seven sacred rivers, seven sacred cities, and seven sacred places.

Seven is perfection and completion; there are seven marriage vows and seven steps the couple must make together.

Seven is perfection and completion; if God wants us to be together, nothing can separate us. We have seven years!

Seven is perfection and completion; there are seven wedding vows, seven steps taken together, and marriage lasts seven lifetimes.

Come, My Love

Let us walk the gardens where fragrant blossoms grow.
Let us admire the radiant colors and feel their soft petals on our skin.
The grape blossoms have opened, the fragrant cherry and apple blossoms are in bloom.
There I will give you my love, which I have held captive for you.

17 July 2014

Kale!

I am bahut Kale, but bahut lovely.
Don't stare at me because I am dark.
I am kissed by the sun.

Kiss me with the kisses of your lips, my love.
Your kisses are sweeter than the juice of a pomegranate
Your hands embrace me, I am weak with love

I am bahut Kale, but bahut lovely.
Don't stare at me because I am dark.
I am kissed by the sun.

Dekho! There he stands
His stature as the majestic palms
Come, let me see your face.
Let me hear your sweet voice.

I am bahut Kale, but bahut lovely.
Don't stare at me because I am dark.
I am kissed by the sun.

You whom my soul loves
Lay your head on my breasts
Your fragrance is of myrrh
Come to my garden.

I am bahut Kale, but bahut lovely.
Don't stare at me because I am dark.
I am kissed by the sun.

My beloved has come to my garden
The North and South winds are aroused
Blow upon my garden,
Let its fragrant spices flow.

17 July 2014

Even after She's Gone

Even after she's gone, I am learning from her.
As I recall the memories of her
I gain a new understanding.
When I had her I could not understand.
Now sitting in a hair salon of all places,
I have my blinding epiphany!
I recall something she said to me consistently,
I was so angry with her!
Now I am a mother and I do the same thing
I understand the lessons she teaches, even after she's gone.

When I asked her for advice, many times she would say,
"Take it to the Lord in prayer."
All I wanted was for her to tell me what to do!
And so she did.
She taught me to trust in God and not man.
She did it because her answer may not be what God wants.
She was strengthening my relationship with God.
Even after she's gone, she was teaching me
To be intimate with God, she knew that
My personal relationship with God is all that mattered.
And I realize this after she's gone

Awake

To laugh and smile constantly because of you,
one could never believe my good fortune.
I have only dreamed to feel this way,
and I feared it would forever be a dream.
Oh, how you melted my pain away,
or at least numbed it while I smiled.
I was certainly not ready for love,
even though I thought I was when I spoke with you.
Aaagh! You made me feel so sweet, so special,
when I had been raped and robbed of beauty.
You know, I was happy to feel for you from behind my scene.
You would never have known.
I never imagined you cared for me too.
Why? Why did you have to tell me? And why did I agree?
At this point I wish you never said a word.
You should have left us as we were.
Just friends!
You said you were afraid to hurt me,
so many times you said you would not leave.
You wanted me to leave, but you did not know I was stubborn too,
did you? DID YOU!
You! Awakened love with in me.
You said you chose to love me, and if you can't love me
for my kindness you would find something else.
But it must be a lie, because you don't love me anymore!
I hate you! Your words were so perfect!

They healed me! But your actions have broken me again.
Oh, God! I hate you! It pains in my soul,
so much that I can't let you go!
And I want to! But the sutures from this wound are not yet healed.
To pull them out prematurely
 will leave me open and susceptible to infection.
So I shall patiently nurse this, with love and care.
I hate that I my heart was broken again,
but I am proud of my heart because somehow it still works.
You gave me love, the kind of cognizant love,
beyond words and feelings.
I am proud to say I love you! But I am even more proud to know
that know exactly what it means.

08 September 2014

Last Love, First Laugh

Last love, I do remember you
through the turbulent billowing of my chaotic mind
Our passionate embraces do bring me
to a joyful place in this my old age
I smile as I reminisce on your lovely and languid gaze,
The deep personal silence between us echoes with sensual resolve
What shall we do, my enamored sage?
Shall we indulge in this wildly titillating invitation
to play uninhibited and free? Shall we, my love?
First Laugh, I cling to you as desperately as I can, for I certainly
long for your return
The first time I saw your physical embodiment, I saw the finger-
prints of God
As though He played joyfully in the clay
that formed you and willfully left perfect imperfections
I lived each touch, I breathed consciously in the sensation of feel-
ing, my fingers traced your brow bone I laughed boldly, richly,
deeply, as I realized the explosive magnitude of the moment
It was an intoxicating laugh, the sound of it made you drunk with
adoration for me
And I relished the only moment I shared with my last love and our
first laugh.

15 October 2014
Healing happiness joy, blue swami J
The journey unconditional love support positivity

Follow Through

Aloha!

"I got so much things to say right now, I got so much things to say." That's the Ziggy Marley song dancing precariously in my head right now. Today I feel so content and happy, but my mind is so busy, and yet I am used to it now. In the maddening tornado of randomly strung together thoughts swirling in my cranium, I manage to pluck out the "important" thoughts, things that are priority and need to be addressed near term or now. Imagine if you will, Dorothy with a butterfly net trying to catch beautiful sapphire butterflies while being tossed violently around in (what else but...) the perpetual tornado that lands her in Oz. That's my mind every day. Every day I fight to make sense out of nonsense. Some days it's easier than others.

So it's not that you aren't motivated to get something done; it's that you are not ready to completely commit to it. It's really about generating enough action potential to force an action. Sounds weird, huh? Okay, let me try again.... Let me give a visual ;). Imagine that you want to quit smoking. You definitely know it is bad for you. You are totally motivated! You may have even quit a few times but fell off course due to some extenuating circumstance(s). Understand that it's not lack of motivation; it's your mind! Your mind is your biggest roadblock! Even though it is your mind that has you motivated to quit in the first place. Your mind is (excuse my language) a lazy sack of (whatever word you want to use) crap! It will tell you logically you need to quit smoking and in the same breath argue with you about the ten billion more important things you need to accomplish before you can even start to quit!

So let me give a few pointers to help you with follow-through. SIDEBAR: Some of these are much harder to do than others!

1. Accountability Partner: Find someone (or several someones) who is willing to commit with you on your goal. You are less likely to give excuses to someone who is holding your feet to the fire.

2. Tell your mind to STFU: I know! That's so rude, right? Well, your mind is keeping you from bettering yourself, so I think it's an appropriate command! Remember: "They are just thoughts; you don't have to buy into them." You tell your mind what to do, turn off the thoughts, ignore them! Think less and just do! (Nike: Just Do It!)

3. Write it down and be VERY Specific: Give yourself explicit instructions, the five W's (who, what, where, when, and why). I will quit smoking by not purchasing cigarettes, starting 0600, Monday, 10 October 2014...write a plan on how you will quit and your contingencies for cravings, etc.

4. Discipline yourself: Eventually this will become second nature for you. Your mind will stop arguing with you as your actions become habit.

P.S.: If you have not read the book *Switch* by Chip and Dan Heath, I recommend it! Why? Because it is all about CHANGE. How to make changes not just in the workplace but in your personal life. It provides explanations on why change is so difficult (change = follow-through).

And it provides a "how-to" framework on making change possible. Direct the Rider, Motivate the Elephant, and Set the Path.

P.S.S.: I just love the fact that there are several ways to state the same thing. Even if one does not click with you right away, the other might. And the best part?! Well, that's when you understand the concept no matter which way it is presented. I get so excited.

The Gateway to India

Honestly, I cared for the significance of the historical monument, but I cared more that she was there with me.

Secretly, I wanted to touch her, though she was not mine to touch, to feel her bones, her skin, her hairs, if only for a gentle grazing of my fingertips in passing. I wanted to run my fingers through her hair, even count her grays, as though they could enumerate her hardships. The scars on her face, I wanted to pass my fingers back and forth over them; something about her scars intrigued me. I wanted to kiss her face, maybe to show her that I cared, for some kind of respect, or in hopes that she would accept me as well. I wanted to wrap my arms around her waist, and bury my face in her bosom, and breathe her in, because it would be our only real moment together.

Written by me...just now, because I was moved to do so.
Love, Debbie Smith

She Just Looks Like a Dreamer

For whatever reason, she just looks like a dreamer. She always has this "far-off" look. It's severely evident in her work; she is always late, never knows what is actually happening now. I am surprised she knows anything at all. She takes mental vacations more than anyone I know. It seems she longs to escape her life. Well, the reality of it all, my love, is that you have the choice. Your life is concurrent to the choices you make in any given situation. Your dreams are your own. If you chose to. She seems to be just now understanding just how powerful she really is.

She is becoming self-empowered.

My Next Adventure

I am such a busybody. I am reading *Retire Young Retire Rich* by Robert Kiyosaki and *Lean In* by Sheryl Sandberg, and also I am listening to Deepak Chopra's audio book titled *The Book of Secrets*. And I am in the process of planning my next adventure to India.

I am completely excited at the prospects of my near future. Financial freedom is only a few smart decisions and a promotion away. After years of making stupid financial choices based on impulse, I am finally at a place where I can turn that around and get on the "upswing." I need to educate myself on finances and teach my teenager the things I am learning. I must set him up for success at an early age. My biggest issue is I can lead a boy to water, but he won't drink unless he is thirsty.

The Elevation of a Flower

I sat on a bad impression AstroTurf, serving as a floor mat outside of a Tibetan jewelry store. The rain came in from seemingly nowhere to wash away the beauty of a bright, sunny day. Or wash away the bad luck of no sales and slow business or refresh and renew life on every level. Honestly, it's all in how it is perceived, how God's gift of the rain is received by each of us. I was indifferent to it, but I was very mildly annoyed at the small stream of dirty, red, muddy water, making its way down the narrow street, the street that brought life, business, and money, to merchants, became still, barely alive, humbled as nature forced all to pay homage. Some enjoyed the rest, others tried to escape it; and still some tried to hurry it along. The street was sandwiched by merchant shops and shacks on one side filled with cheaply made clothes and gifts. If you have seen one, you have seen them all, the difference being the people, their stories, all different but similar, their goals all the same, money, business, and at any lie worth telling. On the other side of the street, a beautiful cliff dropped somewhat dramatically into the ocean, with lush, green shrubbery, vines, and jutting rocks adorning the cliff face. But also like acne on a handsome adolescent boy's face, trash, plastic, old food, and scraps dotted the cliff face as well. This was my only disappointment. Man had spoiled the beauty of the place with their disregard. The irony, locals sell the beauty of the land to nature-loving foreigners, yet they themselves make it ugly and charge a high price. Like a whore, ill treated by her pimp, used by her customers, and lonely, for no one truly loves her. I held the deep pink hibiscus flower in my hand only then. Fifteen minutes prior to that, it had adorned my hair, and I smiled as brightly as the sun shined. Though a small cloud threatened my sunny joy with the idea, they (my complimentors) were laughing at me; I was the only one with a pretty flower in my hair. Despite the thought I kept smiling, kept my flower, and kept walking. Then down came the rain, beating on my head, my hair soaking in each pelting raindrop. There was no protection for the flower that adorned my hair. It looked withered, as I walked past a mirrored window and noticed my reflection. I knew I had doomed that flower to a shorter lifespan once I plucked it from the life-giving branch to adorn my hair, which was already beautifully unique because of my braids. The likes of which are rare in these parts the world.

I pulled the weather-beaten flower from my hair and placed it in my purse. As I paused on the plastic rubbery floor mat off the Tibetan jewelry shop, I noticed a shopkeeper next to me, slim build, sun-kissed complexion, low hair, and obviously not local. He migrated from Tibet to make money as a fisherman and his mature and handsome features, including his wedding band, suggested he was well, married with children. His brother appeared opposite (though not in their body, which was similar). Long hair, carefree look, T-shirt and shorts, smiling readily. He was impatient and obviously good looking. His slanted eyes, elevated cheekbones, and moderately full lips, darkened by smoking, were all animated when he spoke and smiled. He was darker than his brother, which led me to believe he was the fisherman. There was a third brother, who was very tall, with very large feet (could he have belonged to the milkman?) He seemed awkward, as though of his abnormal height (abnormal, only because he was a palm tree amongst a sea of shorts) kept him from venturing out often, due to too many tiny shrubs staring up at him a condemning/critical side eye. Either way, I thought he was too beautiful to look at, and entirely too elusive (side note: He had a deep, melodious, and low bellowing voice; it sent positive vibrations erupting through my sternum).

I played with my technology, something that was seemingly quite out of place in this natural, serene part of the world, but I had a desire to capture the moment. The moment of two brothers playing in a stream of muddy red water. It was almost a dance between these two adult men. I imaginatively dubbed them long (for long hair), short (for short hair), and tall (for the tallest). Secretly, or so I thought, I snapped pictures with my camera/Smartphone of the two. Long, anxiously sweeping water with his feet down the cliff side, as if helping nature's process flow smoothly with close of the heaven and cause the source to dry up—it didn't. Short joined in from his shop that as a tethered to his empty fish stand, he didn't venture too far from it—stable, secure. Tall had briefly come out of hiding to head up the street. Long choreograph action on the flip side, moving toward and away from the shop that I, constantly in motion and constant sweeping water away. I observed all, though at the time I was smitten by Long's hair and wild at heart features.

I removed my hibiscus from the protection of my purse, disgusted with it, fed up and wondering why I even plucked it from its branch. I tossed it from me, just a few inches away. I took a picture of it, then I took it again in my hand. I thought maybe there was hope for the dying flower as the subject of a photograph or even a poem, or maybe this essay/short story. I tossed it farther out, hoping it would be caught up in a stream of mud. A thing of beauty, spending its dying moments making its filthy, wretched environment more beautiful. The flower fell a few feet (maybe one and a half feet) short of the stream and doomed to a new fate. I snapped another picture.

I didn't believe anyone noticed or cared that I had discarded my flower; I considered reaching for it again and placing it in the stream. As the flower lay in its abyss, lost between a disparaged ending and a new beginning, the flower, the thing of beauty, was gently picked up by the fish merchant, Short. He gave the flower to Long the rugged wonderer, who aptly affixed her atop the sign, which advertised and enticed customers to his place of business. I snapped another picture of the fish merchant delicately handling my once flower and a final shot of her and her resting place, a place of high honor, the place where she would spend the rest of her time as a thing of beauty, making her environment and circumstance beautiful.

Shubhan Allah! The whole thing made me smile; it gave my heart joy as the cycle of life displayed in the span of about forty-five minutes, through a flower; so many of life's themes were addressed in that moment.

Ramjesh

When I am being selfish, I consider no one. I am insensitive and mean. This whole week since I asked you if you loved me, I asked God what to do, how to handle it. I was presented with two choices. The first was do what God does; he loves us even when we reject him, he nurtures and cares for us, he guides us, he is our comfort. This required humility and self-sacrifice. The second was to be proud and full of myself and my feelings, which is easiest for me and anyone else to do. I chose the second option, telling myself that "I am not God, so I don't have to act like Him." But I am not anyone else, and I know that you cannot love me. I don't fully understand it, but I know it is the way that it is. I know it has to do with everything that a man identifies with, being a provider, a protector, and a lover. You were all those things to her, and it meant nothing. She left for someone with more status and money. I don't understand because I am not a man, and it does not resonate with me as much as the need to be loved and protected.

I respect you more than you know! I don't say it often, because there are a lot of men I don't respect. But you, and both my brothers and maybe a handful of men, I respect. Understand that even though you are younger than me, I value your opinion, I think you are wise, I love the questions you ask, I think you are a deep thinker, and I learn from you. Ramuji, the most attractive thing to me is to be able to learn from you. It's probably what keeps me intrigued, and you usually have something new to enlighten me with. I recall you telling me to include Jhordan in the decision-making process of our family and I have. I told Carlo what you said, and he completely agreed with you. You are far more spiritual than you let on. I can only humbly ask for your patience; you are on a journey to finding yourself, but still we are a team. I am on a journey as well, one for patience. I have my moments of weakness, when I turn to God for strength and completely ignore what He has directed me to do, which is to be humble and patient, then I end up here...being humble but with drama attached to it. My fear is not being good enough to be loved; you have tried to build me up, and I know I am good enough. But sometimes my fear gets the best of me.

I ask that you will be patient with me as I learn patience for you (and others). Please continue to accept me and challenge me. Ramuji, you are my perfect-fitting jeans, you are my companion and my friend. God made this journey for us to take separately but together, but he is working a miracle before our very eyes and it will be a testimony to others. That is what I think.

The View

The view from my room. Two seemingly incomplete buildings, one old and forgotten, overtaken by crows and trees. Discarded by man, left in disrepair, weather beaten and reclaimed by nature. Maybe a once beautiful facade of human engineering graced the streets, now its meagre bones lay exposed, like an old beggar on the streets. Just there, still alive and maybe wondering why. Hollow eyes, protruding cheekbones, weak and withered fingers barely cupped in request for spare change. The other a promising creation! And oh! The possibilities. It stands tall and strong, ready to face rain, heat, wind, weight, noise, technology, and possibly be the perch for a masked crusader, vigilant in her search for relentless evildoers. Who knows what lies ahead?

There are no lungis here in Mumbai. And for the first time, I slept the entire night through without waking up to cough. I have no plans for today.

Thank You!

Jhordan K. Walters (the love of my LIFE)

Howard O. E. Smith (my eldest brother, who beat a guy with a tree branch for me)

Carlo Smith (my unofficial shrink, guru, son's uncle-step-up-and-be-a-man-father and sounding board)

Sandria Tugutu (BFF since prep school, prayer warrior, and Mary Kay consultant)

Elizabeth Silva Sampaio (I learned a lot from you about being a human.)

Danique Williams (my adopted sister)

Neville Rose (my military mentor)

All the men and women who broke my heart (You have helped me become who and what I am today.)

Ramuji (my fantastic fellow and loyal friend who was the very last person to tell me I should publish my poems. If you were just being nice, thanks, but there is no turning back now! Muah!)

References

HEATH, C., & HEATH, D. (2010). Switch : how to change things when change is hard. NEW YORK: BROADWAY BOOKS.

JOHNSON, S. (1998). Who moved my cheese? : an amazing way to deal with change in your work and in your life. NEW YORK: PUTNAM.

MARLEY, B. (1977, JUNE 3). I GOT SO MUCH THINGS TO SAY RIGHT NOW. (B. MARLEY, Performer) KINGSTON, JAMAICA.

MCCARTNEY, P., & LENNON, J. (1965, AUGUST 6). YES-TERDAY. (T. BEATLES, Performer) LONDON, ENG-LAND.

MICHALKO, M. (2006). THINKER TOYS. BERKELEY: TEN SPEED PRESS.